Foreword

Shalom! For almost 2,000 years, the synagogue, like the home, has been the center of Jewish life.

Three Hebrew names for "synagogue" describe what goes on in it. We call the synagogue *Beit Tefilah,* a house of prayer. Here people gather to worship, sing praise to God, offer thanks, and ask for help. Wherever Jews gather together, there is a community of prayer. We don't need a special building to pray; we just need each other. Still, Jews have always constructed places to bring people together for prayer.

We call the synagogue *Beit Midrash,* a house of study. In every sanctuary is a book, the Torah. Jews are called the People of the Book. You will often find libraries in synagogues, and you will always find people, young and old, learning.

We call the synagogue *Beit Keneset,* a house of gathering. Actually, the word "synagogue" comes from two Greek words meaning "bringing together." It is where people come during good times and sad times. They mark important moments in life with each other. They come to do good deeds to help others.

In the synagogue you will see people welcome a new child into the community. Here young boys and girls of thirteen become bar and bat mitzvah, accepting their responsibilities to the Jewish people. Often weddings take place in the synagogue as the bride and groom stand under a *chuppah,* a wedding canopy. People also come to remember those they love who have died.

There are many symbols you will see in the synagogue. They help remind us about God, about Torah, and about living a good life. The information you find in this book will help you feel welcome. Come in!

Rabbi Sandy Eisenberg Sasso, D.Min.,
author of *God's Paintbrush, In God's Name,* and
Adam & Eve's First Sunset: God's New Day

Books in the Series

What You Will See Inside…

- *A Synagogue*

- *A Mosque*

- *A Catholic Church*

- *Lo que se puede ver dentro de una iglesia católica*

- *A Hindu Temple*

What You Will See Inside
A SYNAGOGUE

Rabbi Lawrence A. Hoffman
and Dr. Ron Wolfson
with Photographs by Bill Aron

Walking Together, Finding the Way
SKYLIGHT PATHS Publishing
Woodstock, Vermont

For People of All Faiths, All Backgrounds
JEWISH LIGHTS Publishing
Woodstock, Vermont

What You Will See Inside a Synagogue

2004 First Printing
Text © 2004 Lawrence A. Hoffman and Ron Wolfson

For information regarding permission to reprint material from this book, please mail or fax your request in writing to SkyLight Paths Publishing, Permissions Department, at the address / fax number listed below, or e-mail your request to permissions@skylightpaths.com.

Library of Congress Cataloging-in-Publication Data
Hoffman, Lawrence A., 1942–
What you will see inside a synagogue / Lawrence Hoffman and Ron Wolfson.
p. cm. — (What you will see inside—)
ISBN 1-59473-012-1 (hardcover)
1. Judaism—Liturgy—Juvenile literature. 2. Judaism—Customs and practices—Juvenile literature. 3. Fasts and feasts—Judaism—Juvenile literature. 4. Synagogues—Juvenile literature. I. Wolfson, Ron. II. Title. III. Series.
BM660.H635 2004
296.4'6—dc22

2004011178

Grateful acknowledgment is given for permission to reprint images from the following sources: Bill Aron—page 3, page 5, page 6 *(Kippah),* page 7, page 8, page 9, page 10 *(Amidah),* page 11, page 12, page 13, page 14 *(Oneg Shabbat),* page 15, page 16, page 17 *(Seder Plate),* page 19, page 20 (bar mitzvah), page 21 *(Mazal Tov),* page 22, page 23, page 24, page 25, page 26, page 27, page 28, page 29, page 30; Richard S. Vosko—page 6 (Lobby, Congregation Immanuel, Denver, Colorado), page 31; Temple Beth-El Zedeck, Indianapolis—page 17 (boy in library), page 18 (soup kitchen); Jules Porter—page 20 (bat mitzvah); Joellyn Wallen Zollman—page 21 *(Chuppah);* Jonathan Kremer—page 21 *(K'tubah);* CCAR Press—page 10 *(Siddur).* Thanks to the following people for providing the photographs on page 4: Corinne Lightweaver (photograph by Stacey B. Peyer), Stuart M. Matlins, Rabbi Angela Warnick Buchdahl (photograph by George Kalinsky), Bill Aron, Rabbi Gershom Sizomu, Sylvia Boorstein, Aaron Bousel, Lauren Seidman (photograph by Michael H. Seidman), Zalman M. Schachter-Shalomi, Ron Wolfson.

Every effort has been made to trace and acknowledge copyright holders of all material used in this book. The publisher apologizes for any errors or omissions that may remain and asks that such be brought to our attention for correction in future editions.

10 9 8 7 6 5 4 3 2 1

Manufactured in China

SkyLight Paths Publishing is creating a place where people of different spiritual traditions come together for challenge and inspiration, a place where we can help each other understand the mystery that lies at the heart of our existence.

SkyLight Paths sees both believers and seekers as a community that increasingly transcends traditional boundaries of religion and denomination—people wanting to learn from each other, *walking together, finding the way.*

Book and Jacket Design: Dawn DeVries Sokol with Bridgett Taylor and Tim Holtz

SkyLight Paths, "Walking Together, Finding the Way" and colophon are trademarks of LongHill Partners, Inc., registered in the U.S. Patent and Trademark Office.

Walking Together, Finding the Way
Published by SkyLight Paths Publishing
A Division of LongHill Partners, Inc.
Sunset Farm Offices, Route 4, P.O. Box 237
Woodstock, VT 05091
Tel: (802) 457-4000   Fax: (802) 457-4004
www.skylightpaths.com

For People of All Faiths, All Backgrounds
Jewish Lights Publishing
A Division of LongHill Partners, Inc.
Sunset Farm Offices, Route 4, P.O. Box 237
Woodstock, VT 05091
Tel: (802) 457-4000   Fax: (802) 457-4004
www.jewishlights.com

Shalom! Welcome!

*"Shalom!"** is a greeting in Hebrew, a holy language for Jews. This book gives you some other Hebrew words for things that you may hear in synagogues. When you see this mark (*), look at the bottom of the page to see how the Hebrew word is pronounced.

Sometimes a synagogue is called a temple, or a *shul,** a word that reminds us of "school," because synagogues are places for learning, not just praying. Learning is a very important part of Judaism.

Synagogues may be big or small, fancy or plain. No matter what they look like, however, all synagogues are places for learning, praying, and gathering together. People gather to celebrate happy times, to find comfort when they are sad, to give charity, and to do good deeds. In this book we focus mainly on the synagogues and services of the Conservative, Reconstructionist, and Reform movements in Judaism, the synagogues that you will see most in North America.

Everyone is welcome here, because Jews believe that every single person is made in God's image. That means that our goodness, our conscience, and our right to be treated with dignity make us like God. Synagogues are holy places, where everyone is welcome because everyone is holy—like God.

The most important room in a synagogue is its sanctuary, where we meet to pray. Mostly, this book shows you what is in the sanctuary. But sanctuaries are not just for things. They need people. So synagogues are for people. The Bible says, "May those who enter be blessed." When you enter a synagogue, we pray that God blesses you.

Welcome to the synagogue!

Shalom: shah-LOHM
Shul: SHOOL

Who Are the Jewish People?

JUDAISM IS A RELIGION, not a race or nationality. There are Jews of many different colors and from many different nations. What binds them together as a people are a shared way of living, beliefs, and rituals.

Gathering for Shabbat

ON WEEKDAYS, THE SYNAGOGUE FILLS WITH PEOPLE attending classes, looking for help, and working on projects. In some synagogues, people come every morning and evening to pray.

On the Sabbath—we call it by its Hebrew name, Shabbat*—and on Jewish holidays, even more people come to pray. When we enter, we stop to talk and greet one another with *Shabbat shalom** ("Have a peaceful Sabbath"), *Chag samei'ach!** ("Happy holiday"), or *Shanah tovah** ("Have a good new year"), depending on the occasion. As people come in, someone who is part of the congregation may welcome them, whether they are Jewish or not, and especially if they have never visited before. Judaism encourages us to welcome strangers.

On the right-hand doorpost of every synagogue is a small decorative container called a *m'zuzah**. It reminds us that this is God's house. People who enter and leave the building may touch the *m'zuzah* with their finger-tips, and then put their fingers to their lips as if offering a kiss, as a sign of respect for God. Each special room in the synagogue (the sanctuary, the classrooms, and the library, for example) may have its own *m'zuzah*.

Jewish homes also have a *m'zuzah*, to remind us that our homes should be filled with love and kindness. A synagogue is like a big Jewish home for all Jews—and for anyone else who wants to visit.

M'ZUZAH: The *m'zuzah* tells us, "This is a holy place." God visits us in our homes, and we visit God in the synagogue.

Shabbat: shah-BAHT
Shabbat shalom: shah-BAHT shah-LOHM
Chag samei'ach: KHAG sah-MAY-akh
Shanah tovah: shah-NAH toh-VAH, or SHAH-nah TOH-vah
M'zuzah: m'-zoo-ZAH, or m'-ZOO-zah
Sh'ma: sh'-MAH

SH'MA: Inside the *m'zuzah* is a handwritten prayer called the *Sh'ma**, a section of the Bible that reminds us to love God, just as God loves us. The main words of the *Sh'ma* are, "Hear O Israel, the Eternal is our God, the Eternal alone."

KIPPAH: Some men and women wear a *kippah*—a special head covering—in the synagogue to show respect for God, and some people wear them all the time.

Preparing for Prayer

TALLIT: Some people wrap themselves in their *tallit*, when they first put it on, to help them concentrate on being with God.

IN SOME SYNAGOGUES, people wear a special head covering, a *kippah**, and a prayer shawl, a *tallit**. The *kippah* is also called a *yarmulke**. Wearing it shows respect for God. The *tallit* comes in many sizes and colors, but it always contains four long knotted fringes (called *tsitsit**) on each corner. Long ago, the Bible says, God rescued Jews from slavery in Egypt. Some people say when Jews look at the fringes, they remember how bad it is to be a slave, and how important it is to treat everyone kindly and with respect.

The *tsitsit* are arranged so that they add up to the number of *mitzvot**, or commandments, God has told us to do. When we look at the *tsitsit*, we are reminded to do what God asks of us.

In some synagogues (called Orthodox), the *kippah* and *tallit* are usually worn only by men. In other synagogues (called Reform, Conservative, and Reconstructionist), women frequently wear them too.

The people you see here have just arrived and are getting ready to enter the sanctuary, which is through the open doorway. Each is getting a prayer book, called a *siddur**. Then they might put on a *tallit*. Some people wear a *kippah* all the time, not just in the synagogue, because God is everywhere.

Kippah: kee-PAH
Tallit: tah-LEET
Yarmulke: YAHR-mul-kuh
Tsitsit: tsee-TSEET
Mitzvot: meets-VOHT
Siddur: see-DOOR, or SIH-d'r
T'fillin: t'FILL-in

T'FILLIN: At prayer services in the morning, some people wear *t'fillin**, small boxes that are placed on the forehead (next to the brain) and on the inside of the upper arm (next to the heart)—the places where we think and feel. The boxes are held in place by leather straps, tied in the shape of the Hebrew letters that spell God's name. Like the *m'zuzah*, the boxes hold the prayer we call the *Sh'ma*.

TSITSIT: Specially knotted fringes on the four corners of the *tallit* also remind us of the "four corners of the earth" where all God's people live.

INSIDE THE ARK: When the ark is opened, you can see the many Torah scrolls standing beside one another, each dressed in a special covering and decorated with silver crowns and plates.

The Holiest Place in the Synagogue

FOR JEWS, THE HOLIEST BOOK IN THE WORLD is the Hebrew Bible. The holiest part of the Hebrew Bible is its first part, the five books of Moses, which we call the Torah. It tells the story of how our ancestors first met God and found out how God wants us to live.

The Torah is handwritten in beautifully decorated Hebrew letters on a material called parchment, which is rolled up into a scroll. The Torah scrolls are kept in an ark, a cabinet at the front of the sanctuary. The ark is the holiest place in the synagogue. It usually holds many Torah scrolls. Jews treat Torah scrolls so carefully and with such respect that they can be used over and over again for hundreds of years.

BIMAH: The area where the people who lead the prayers stand. In some synagogues, the *bimah* is in the middle of the sanctuary instead of at the front.

Above the ark is a *ner tamid**, an "eternal light" that shines day and night to symbolize God's presence. The ark is usually on the eastern wall, so that during prayer, Jews can face the ark and Jerusalem, the city that Jews consider the holiest place on earth.

In front of the ark is the *bimah**. It is the raised platform where the people who lead prayers usually stand. Sometimes it has a candle-holder called a *m'norah**. The one you see in the picture holds seven candles, just like the *m'norah* that the Israelites of the Bible made. The *bimah* may have other things, too, like an eight-branched *m'norah* that is used on the holiday of Chanukah and is sometimes called a *chanukiyah**; a six-pointed Jewish star, called *magen david**, the "star of David," named after King David of the Bible; or decorations shaped like a lion, called Lion of Judah, the sign for a biblical tribe (where the name "Judaism" comes from). Look also for flags of the country where you live, and of Israel, the Jewish "homeland," where most of the Bible stories happened.

SHABBAT CANDLES: In Judaism, each new day begins at sundown and continues through the next morning and afternoon. Saturday is a holy day—the Sabbath, called Shabbat. On Friday night, when it begins, you may see someone on the *bimah* lighting two Shabbat candles to bring the light of Shabbat joy to people.

Ner tamid: NAYR tah-MEED   *M'norah:* m'NOH-rah, or m'-noh-RAH   *Magen david:* mah-GAYN dah-VEED
Bimah: BEE-mah   *Chanukiyah:* khah-noo-ki-YAH

How Jews Pray

JEWS PRAY DIRECTLY TO GOD, but our prayers are usually led by two people: a cantor (called *chazan** in Hebrew) and a rabbi. They are called messengers of the congregation because they help direct our prayers to God. The cantor sings or chants melodies that reflect the mood of the service. The rabbi reads the prayers aloud, and teaches about Judaism by giving a sermon during the service. All Jews are encouraged to learn how to lead prayers, however, and anyone can become a rabbi or cantor. The Hebrew word *rabbi* means "teacher."

Do you remember the name of the prayer book? It is called a *siddur*, which means "order." The prayer service has an order to it and is often read in Hebrew, the ancient language of the Bible.

During a service, we usually sit, but we sometimes stand, especially during a prayer called the *Amidah**, when people may pray silently or in a whisper, as if personally "standing before God."

In some synagogues, musical instruments are played.

Chazan: chaz-ZAHN, or CHAH-z'n
Amidah: ah-MEE-dah, or ah-mee-DAH
Davening: DAH-v'ning

These are duties whose worth cannot be measured:
honoring one's father and mother,
acts of love and kindness,
diligent pursuit of knowledge and wisdom,
hospitality to strangers,
visiting the sick,
celebrating with bride and groom,
consoling the bereaved,
praying with sincerity,
and making peace where there is strife.
And the study of Torah leads to them all.

אֵלוּ דְבָרִים שֶׁאֵין לָהֶם שָׁעוּר:
כִּבּוּד אָב וָאֵם,
וּגְמִילוּת חֲסָדִים,
וְהַשְׁכָּמַת בֵּית הַמִּדְרָשׁ
שַׁחֲרִית וְעַרְבִית,
וְהַכְנָסַת אוֹרְחִים,
וּבִקוּר חוֹלִים,
וְהַכְנָסַת כַּלָּה,
וּלְוָיַת הַמֵּת,
וְעִיּוּן תְּפִלָּה,
וַהֲבָאַת שָׁלוֹם בֵּין אָדָם
לַחֲבֵרוֹ.
וְתַלְמוּד תּוֹרָה כְּנֶגֶד כֻּלָּם.

SIDDUR: This *siddur* is open at a prayer that people say together. In this prayer book, Hebrew and English appear on both pages, and people pray mostly in English. Sometimes people pray entirely in Hebrew.

AMIDAH: The whole congregation stands to say the *Amidah* (the "standing prayer"). Sometimes the cantor sings part of it out loud. Often the people join in, as they do with many parts of the service that are sung. In some synagogues, the people read a prayer by *davening** it—that is, they all read it aloud, but by themselves, not all together. It sounds like mumbling, but really they are praying to God at their own speed, starting all together and then waiting until everyone finishes, before the cantor sings the last few lines and everyone begins again at the next paragraph.

Reading the Torah

ON SHABBAT AND HOLIDAYS—and on Mondays and Thursdays, too—someone reads part of the Torah scroll out loud. Each week, a different part is read; then the Torah is rolled forward for the next week, until, at the end of a year, we read the last little bit and then roll it back to the beginning and start all over again.

Whenever we read Torah, we remove it from the ark with great respect, and parade through the congregation holding it. The tiny bells that are part of its covering jingle as the parade moves through the synagogue. People crowd into the aisles to get close enough to the scroll to kiss it by touching it with the fringes of the *tallit* (the *tsitsit*), a prayer book, or even their fingers. Then they kiss whatever they used to touch it, to show their love for Torah. The Torah is then placed upon a special reading table, sometimes in the middle of the congregation, where its cover and ornaments are removed, so that someone can read from it.

YAD: As a sign of respect for the Torah, and to make sure the letters aren't blurred by touching them with fingers, the Torah reader keeps place with a pointer shaped like a human hand at the end. It is called a *yad**, the Hebrew word for "hand."

People from the congregation take turns standing beside the person reading Torah. They say prayers to thank God for giving us the Torah on Mount Sinai. This is called an *aliyah**. When the reading is finished, someone holds the Torah up high so everyone can see its writing, and someone else puts the Torah covering and decorations back on. Sometimes, the Torah is then paraded once again through the congregation before being put back in the ark.

Aliyah: ah-LEE-yah, or ah-lee-YAH
Yad: YAHD
Hakafah: hah-kah-FAH
Simchat Torah: sim-KHAT toh-RAH

HAKAFAH: The parade through the congregation is called a *hakafah**. At an autumn holiday called Simchat Torah*, we finish reading the Torah and then begin it all over again. The Torah parade that day is especially joyous. Children wave flags, and people lead the way dancing around the room, while carrying the Torah.

TORAH SCROLL: Before the Torah is put back in the ark, someone shows the congregation its beautiful writing. It is handwritten by someone specially trained to make every letter perfectly. Many of the letters are decorated.

Enjoying Shabbat

AT THE CONCLUSION OF THE SHABBAT SERVICE IN THE SANCTUARY, everyone is invited to another room to celebrate together at the *Oneg Shabbat**. *Oneg* means "joy." *Oneg Shabbat* means "enjoying Shabbat."

The *Oneg Shabbat* starts with the *Kiddush**, a prayer over wine or grape juice, followed by a blessing over a bread called a *challah**. If it is a Friday evening service, the *Oneg Shabbat* will probably have a large dessert table. Saturday morning prayer services are usually followed with lunch or just a snack. Some people call it a *kiddush*, after the name of the prayer with which it begins.

Jews believe that God wants us to do certain things called "commandments," not just the Ten Commandments, but many more. Each one is called a mitzvah*. All together, they are called *mitzvot*. It is a mitzvah to attend synagogue prayer services on Shabbat and holidays. It is also a mitzvah to eat together afterward. Mitzvah has also come to mean "good deed."

Oneg Shabbat: OH-neg shah-BAHT
Kiddush: kee-DOOSH, or KIH-dish
Challah: KHAH-lah, or khah-LAH
Mitzvah: meets-VAH, or MITS-vah

KIDDUSH CUP: Over the centuries, Jews have made beautiful wine cups, usually of silver, and used them to celebrate holy days like Shabbat. Some synagogues have small museums or showcases with *kiddush* cups and other things that you see in this book.

SHARING THE *CHALLAH*: Sometimes people simply cut the *challah* in slices before eating it, but the people here are having fun as they get ready to tear off a piece for each person.

***CHALLAH* PLATE:** This special plate is decorated with Hebrew letters.

***CHALLAH* COVER:** The *challah* on this plate has a decorated cover. This one says (in Hebrew) "Jerusalem."

TALMUD: The Talmud has more than a thousand pages just like this one. The main reading is in the middle of the page. Comments by readers who lived hundreds of years ago are printed all around the borders. People study the center first, and then read the comments around the page. Some Jews try to study a different page every day. Others study just one page for many days. Studying Talmud is for advanced students; it is like going to "Jewish college."

Prayer and Learning Go Together

WE SOMETIMES PRAY NOT JUST IN THE SANCTUARY, but in other rooms too—especially the synagogue library, where this boy is standing. He may have just finished praying there with the adults and other children. If so, a Torah scroll was probably moved there so it could be read during the prayers.

Because the synagogue is a place of Jewish learning—not just prayer—the synagogue library, which has many books about Judaism, is a very important place. Some people spend Shabbat afternoon taking a class there—in the Bible, perhaps, or the Talmud,* a big set of books on almost every Jewish subject, written more than a thousand years ago, and almost as holy to us as our Bible.

People can pray in the library, but also study in the sanctuary. The synagogue also has classrooms where everyone (not just children) can learn about Judaism. They know that in Judaism, learning is as important as prayer.

Talmud: TAHL-m'd
Pesach: PEH-sakh
Seder: SAY-d'r

SEDER PLATE: Most synagogues have a gift shop where people can buy ritual objects for their home. We use this plate on the holiday of Passover, or Pesach*. Passover celebrates the time long ago when God freed our ancestors from slavery in Egypt. The seder plate holds special kinds of food that we use for a Passover dinner called a Seder*. If you are invited to a Seder, look for the special foods there, and ask someone to explain them to you.

Fixing the World

A JEWISH STORY SAYS THAT when God created the world, something went wrong. God sent light throughout the universe, but it got mixed with darkness. Ever since then, we try to rescue the light from the darkness. We call that *tikkun olam**, "fixing the world." We fix the world by doing good deeds, like preparing food for a soup kitchen. We go to synagogues not just for ourselves, but to help others. Some synagogues even open up at night to let homeless people stay there.

Synagogues are like repair shops for the people in our world who are broken. We say that all human beings are partners with God in creation. God started creation, but we have to finish it by fixing God's world.

Tikkun olam: tee-KOON oh-LAHM
Tzedakah: ts'-dah-KAH, or ts'-DAH-kah

TZEDAKAH: Jews are supposed to give charity every day, so after prayer, everyone may contribute money for good causes. It may be collected in a tzedakah* box like this one. *Tzedakah* means "doing the right thing." By giving money to those in need, we help fix the world.

Bar and Bat Mitzvah ...

JEWS GO TO THE SYNAGOGUE to celebrate important times in their lives. At about the thirteenth birthday, a boy becomes a bar mitzvah and a girl becomes a bat mitzvah.

At their bar or bat mitzvah ceremony, we recognize that they are becoming independent teenagers. They are not yet fully grown up, but starting then, they can practice being adults, because they are old enough to be responsible for what they do. When they come to the synagogue on their bar or bat mitzvah day, they are treated like adults. They will already have studied how to lead Jewish lives, and learned how to read Hebrew, so that when they become a

bar mitzvah or a bat mitzvah, they are allowed (for the very first time) to lead the congregation in prayer— the way the rabbi and cantor usually do. The best moment comes when they read the Torah themselves, and the rabbi asks God to bless them.

Family and friends come from all over to witness the ceremony and participate in this passing along of Jewish tradition. The boys and girls are now ready to join the synagogue youth group. If they continue their Jewish studies, they may graduate in a synagogue ceremony called confirmation.

... And Weddings, Too

Jews have everyday names, and special Hebrew names as well. Children do not remember it, but as babies, they were probably given Hebrew names at a ceremony in a synagogue. When they're grown up, they may get married in a synagogue, too.

A Jewish wedding often takes place in the synagogue sanctuary, under a canopy called a *chuppah**. The *chuppah* represents the new home that the bride and groom will make together. It is open on all sides to show that their home will be open to guests, and even to strangers, whom they will welcome.

Chuppah: khoo-PAH, or KHUH-pah
Mazal tov: MAH-z'l TOV
K'tubah: k'-TOO-bah

CHUPPAH: The Jewish wedding canopy represents the new home that the bride and groom will make together.

MAZAL TOV: The wedding ends by the groom stamping on a glass so that it shatters. Even in this moment of their own great happiness, the couple knows that other people in the world are sick and suffering—broken, like the glass—and needing help that the bride and groom promise to give them. When the glass breaks, everyone in the room shouts *"Mazal tov*,"* the Hebrew way of saying, "Congratulations!"

K'TUBAH: The bride and groom have had a *k'tubah**, a specially designed marriage certificate, made for them. This one is decorated with images of Jerusalem.

Celebrating Holidays

WE CELEBRATE JEWISH HOLIDAYS at home and in the synagogue. Chanukah* lasts eight days and is a lot of fun, because we play games with a spinning top called a *dreidel**, and we eat special foods like potato pancakes called *latkes** and doughnuts called *sufganiyot**. People give each other Chanukah presents and say "Happy Chanukah!"

The most important moment comes every evening, when we say prayers, sing songs, and light candles on the special Chanukah *m'norah* that some Jews call a *chanukiyah*. On the first night, we light one candle, using another candle called the *shamash** to light it. Each night, we add a candle, until, by the last night, all eight candles (and the *shamash*, which makes nine) shine brightly. We put the *m'norah* in the window, and light up the darkness outside.

PURIM: Like Chanukah, Purim* too is a holiday for fun. Many people, especially children, come to the synagogue in costume to remember a time when the Jews of Persia escaped a terrible danger. We read the *m'gillah**, a scroll that tells the biblical story of a brave Jewish woman named Esther. Esther saved her people from Haman, an evil man who wanted to kill all the Jews. When the name "Haman" is read aloud, everyone boos and makes noise with a special noise-maker called a *gragger**. Can you imagine booing in a sanctuary!?

GRAGGER: A *gragger* is used to make noise during the Purim story.

Chanukah is celebrated to remember how God saved the Jewish People from an evil king, long ago. The bright lights remind everyone that God helps us in times of darkness.

CHANUKIYAH: A *m'norah* with nine candles used to celebrate Chanukah.

DREIDELS: Fancy *dreidels* for Chanukah games. The *dreidel* is spun like a top, and you win or lose depending on which side lands upward. Prizes are often chocolates, sometimes wrapped in gold or silver foil to look like money, and called *gelt**.

Chanukah: KHAH-noo-kah
Dreidel: DRAY-d'l
Latkes: LOT-kes
Sufganiyot: soof-gah-ni-YOHT
Shamash: shah-MAHSH
Gelt: GEHLT
Purim: POO-rim, or poo-REEM
M'gillah: m'GIH-lah, or m'gee-LAH
Gragger: GRAH-g'r

The High Holy Days

DURING THE FALL, we celebrate two holidays called the High Holy Days. Almost all Jews come to synagogue for these joyous—but very serious—days of reflection. We think about our behavior in the past year, ask for forgiveness of God and each other, and promise to do better in the year ahead. The rabbi and the cantor wear white robes, and even the Torah scrolls are dressed in white, because white is a symbol of fresh starts. As symbols of their new beginning, some people buy new clothes to wear then.

ROSH HASHANAH AND YOM KIPPUR PRAYERS: On Rosh Hashanah and Yom Kippur, people think about how they acted the past year, pray for forgiveness, and look forward to the year ahead.

First comes Rosh Hashanah*, the Jewish New Year. We pray for a blessed and successful year, and we blow a *shofar*, a ram's horn, as a "wake-up call" to remind us to try to be good people. Synagogue prayers often include a choir singing beautiful music. People wish each other "*Shanah tovah*—Have a good year." Some people add, "Have a good and *sweet* year." Happy New Year!

ROSH HASHANAH APPLES AND HONEY: We eat apples dipped in honey, because we hope we will have a sweet year.

Yom Kippur*, the most holy day of the Jewish year, comes ten days later. It begins with a sundown service called *Kol Nidre*, named after the most important prayer of the evening. We go home to sleep but return the next morning for a whole day of prayer. In order to concentrate on our prayers for forgiveness, adults and teenagers fast all day. That means we do not eat or drink anything. Children too may try to fast for a while, if they wish to. When Yom Kippur ends, we return home from the synagogue to "break the fast" and enjoy a festive meal.

Rosh Hashanah: ROSH-hah-SHAH-nah, or ROSH hah-shah-NAH
Shofar: sho-FAR
Yom Kippur: yohm kee-POOR, or yohm KIH-p'r
Kol Nidre: KOHL need-RAY; or kohl NID-ray

BLOWING THE *SHOFAR*: This man has even his head wrapped in a big white *tallit*. You cannot see his face because he is facing away from you, so that he can look at the ark and the Torah scrolls while he blows the *shofar*.

Showing Our Thanks

FIVE DAYS AFTER YOM KIPPUR, we show our thanks to God in a harvest holiday called Sukkot*.

Long ago, our ancestors who were farmers built small huts in their fields during the harvest season. They stayed there day and night while gathering their crops. Today, we too build a temporary outdoor hut called a *sukkah**. It is decorated with tree branches, garden vegetables hung up on string, and, sometimes, the New Year greeting cards that we received for Rosh Hashanah.

After prayer services, we go to the *sukkah* for the *kiddush*. Even though people build a *sukkah* in their synagogue, many families build one at home, outdoors—in their yard, perhaps, or on the roof of their apartment building—so they can see the sky just the way the farmers long ago must have. Some people eat all their meals and even sleep in their *sukkah*.

Sukkot is a holiday of hospitality. "Pretend guests," like the great men and women of the Bible, are invited to visit. Real guests come to eat there also. If you are invited to a *sukkah*, you can bring something to hang up as part of the decoration.

During Sukkot prayer services, we use a *lulav** and an *etrog**. The *lulav* is a bundle of branches from trees that are mentioned in the Bible. They grow in Israel, but, depending on where you live, they might also grow in your backyard. The *etrog* is a fruit that looks like a lemon. People hold these objects together and wave them in all four directions, thanking God for making things grow all over the world.

Sukkot: soo-KOHT
Sukkah: soo-KAH, or SUH-kah
Lulav: LOO-lahv, or loo-LAHV
Etrog: ET-rohg, or et-ROHG

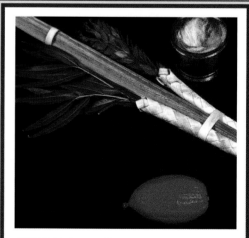

LULAV AND ETROG: The *lulav* is made of branches from trees mentioned in the Bible. We buy a new *lulav* and *etrog* every year, looking for the most beautiful ones we can find, to say, "Thank you, God, for giving us food."

MEMORIAL WALL: This synagogue has many plaques with the names of people who have died. On Yom Kippur, all the lights are lit.

How We Remember

REMEMBERING OUR PAST IS VERY IMPORTANT TO JEWS. On one of the walls of most synagogues, you will find rows of small metal signs. On them are shown the names of people in our families who have died. They are called memorial plaques. Often, there is a small light bulb next to the name, which is lighted on the anniversary of a person's death. That day, relatives of the person who died come to the synagogue to say a prayer called the *Kaddish** and to remember the person. On Yom Kippur, when the synagogue is packed with people, all the lights are lit. We also light *yahrtzeit** candles at home to remember people in our own family who have died. *Yahrtzeit* means the anniversary of the time when people we remember died.

YAHRTZEIT CANDLES: This *yahrtzeit* candle glows brightly all day and all night, even in the darkness, to remind us that people who we loved but who have died can still shine brightly in our memory.

In the synagogue, we remember good times and bad. There was a terrible time called the Holocaust. The Hebrew name for Holocaust is *Sho'ah**. It was a time when some evil people called the Nazis killed six million Jewish children, women, and men in Europe. A day of remembrance called Yom Hasho'ah* brings Jews to the synagogue to remember that terrible time.

But mostly, we remember good people and think about the times when they were still living. We also honor people who are still alive by remembering all the good things they have done. Some synagogues have pictures of the people who were their rabbis and leaders, and sometimes there are pictures of confirmation classes from the past.

Remember the young people becoming bar mitzvah and bat mitzvah? If they help the synagogue when they grow up, they may some day have their pictures on a wall of their synagogues.

Kaddish: KAH-dish, or kah-DEESH
Yahrtzeit: YAHR-tsite, or YOHR-tsite
Sh'oah: SHOH-ah
Yom Hasho'ah: YOM hah-SHOH-ah

ADAT SHALOM—LOS ANGELES, CALIFORNIA

ANSHE SFARD—NEW ORLEANS, LOUISIANA

TEMPLE BETH ISRAEL—BILOXI, MISSISSIPPI

L'hitra'ot. Come again.

THERE ARE MANY SYNAGOGUES ALL OVER THE WORLD. You can find one wherever Jews have lived—and that is just about everywhere! Synagogues are all different, but in many ways they are also the same. They are different because Jews live in different places and build synagogues that reflect their lives. They are the same because all synagogues are spiritual places for Jews—holy places for praying to God, studying the Torah, and doing good deeds.

The Hebrew word for "Goodbye" is *L'hitra'ot**. It means, "See you again!"

So: *L'hitra'ot!* Come again to visit us.

L'hitra'ot: l'-hit-rah-OHT

BETH ELOHIM—CHARLESTON, SOUTH CAROLINA

GATES OF THE GROVE SYNAGOGUE—EAST HAMPTON, NEW YORK

CENTRAL SYNAGOGUE—NEW YORK, NEW YORK

GROWING UP IN THE THIRTIES

Rebecca Hunter

HODDER
Wayland

an imprint of Hodder Children's Books

Produced for Hodder Wayland by
Discovery Books Ltd
Unit 3, 37 Watling Street, Leintwardine, Shropshire SY7 0LW, England

First published in 2001 by Hodder Wayland, an imprint of Hodder Children's Books

British Library Cataloguing in Publication Data

Hunter, Rebecca, 1935-
    Growing up in the thirties
    1. Children - Great Britain - Social life and customs -
    Juvenile literature 2. Great Britain - Social conditions -
    20th century - Juvenile literature 3. Great Britain - Social
    life and customs - 1918-1945 - Juvenile literature
    I. Title
    941 ' . 083 ' 0922

    ISBN 0 7502 3358 3

Printed and bound in Grafiasa, Porto, Portugal

Designer: Ian Winton
Editor: Rebecca Hunter

Hodder Children's Books would like to thank the following for the loan of their material:
Birds Eye Wall's Ltd: page 13 (bottom); **Glasgow Museum of Transport**: page 27, 29;
Hulton Getty: page 6 (top), 8, 10 (top) Humphrey Spender, 14 (top) Richards, 15 (top), 16
(bottom), 18 (top), 19 (bottom) Fred Morley, 21 (top), Reg Speller, 30 (top), cover (left);
Lambeth Archives Department: page 6 (bottom); **Museum of Welsh Life**: page 12;
The Advertising Archives: page 11 (top); **The Leicester Mercury**: page 26 (bottom), 28 (top);
The Robert Opie Collection: page 7 (bottom), 9 (top), 20 (right),
21 (bottom), 24 (bottom), cover (centre).

Hodder Children's Books
A division of Hodder Headline Limited
338 Euston Road
London NW1 3BH

CONTENTS

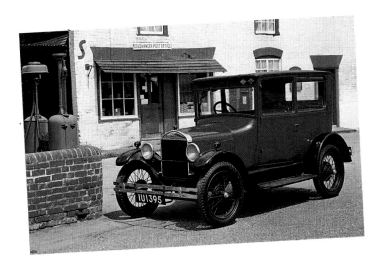

THE 1930s

The 1930s were a time of worldwide recession called the Depression. Many men were unemployed and families had very little money to spend. As if the Depression weren't enough, by the end of the 1930s everyone's lives changed as the Second World War began. In this book, five people who grew up in thirties Britain tell what their lives were like during these difficult times.

NORMAN KIES

Norman was born in 1929 in Central London. His father was a baker and he lived with his parents and sister in South London.

▶ Norman in 1934 aged 5.

BOB DOWNEY

Bob was born in 1924, the youngest of three brothers. His father was a shopkeeper and they lived in Sudbury, a small town in Suffolk.

▶ Bob in 1931 aged 7.

JOYCE BIRD

Joyce grew up in West Ealing, London. She was born in 1923. Her grandfather, father and uncle ran an ironmonger's business with several shops in London.

▶ Joyce in 1935 aged 12.

ARTHUR HOUSTON

Arthur was born in 1928 in Scotland. His father was a solicitor and his mother a doctor. He was the eldest of four children and the family lived in the west end of Glasgow.

▶ Arthur in 1937 aged 9.

SHEILA WALKER

Sheila grew up in a small village in South Wales called Llwynhendy. She was born in 1924 and had two older brothers.

▶ Sheila in 1936 aged 12.

THE DEPRESSION

The Depression was the name given to the early years of the 1930s. It was a time when the country was going through a period of great hardship. Nobody had money to buy goods and many industries suffered. Large numbers of men lost their jobs. Those people who did have jobs worked for very low wages and living conditions were very different from what we are used to today.

Two unemployed men gaze at the factory where they used to work.

HOUSES

Few homes in the thirties had modern conveniences like electric washing machines or refrigerators. Cities were still full of old slum houses with many families living in one-room flats with no indoor bathroom. Most people rented their homes; very few were owned.

THEN & NOW

- The average weekly wage for men in 1938 was £2 13s 3d (£2.66). In 1998 it was £383.

- An average house in the 1930s cost about £800. In 1999 it was £92,500.

Bob

We lived in an old house behind my dad's shop. The house had no bathroom and it only had electricity downstairs. We used candles and oil lights upstairs. There was no central heating or hot water and it was very cold in winter. This picture shows the town of Sudbury where we lived.

Between 1934 and 1939 local councils pulled down over 250,000 slum houses. In their place they built new council housing estates or blocks of flats.

New homes were built in the wealthier suburbs. A typical 1930s house had bay-fronted windows and a garden. For the first time ordinary families were able to borrow money with a mortgage to buy a home of their own.

DAVIS ESTATES LTD

BUILDERS OF HOMES

GAS AND ELECTRICITY

Up until the 1930s, most houses had gas lights, because there was no electricity. The streets were also lit by gas lamps which had to be lit every evening by a lamp lighter.

Arthur

Just before dark the lamp lighter would walk up and down every street lighting the lamps. He carried a long pole with a gas flame at the top. The pole had a lever so that he could open the gas tap. Early in the morning the lamp lighter had to do the rounds again, putting out the lights.

One of the things that changed people's lives most in the 1930s was electricity. A national grid system of cables and pylons was built across the country. Many new power stations were opened. The power stations were powered by coal. By 1937, nine million people had electricity in their homes.

Electricity pylons and cables spread across the countryside.

Electricity made a big difference everywhere. Electric lights replaced gas ones in the streets and traffic lights were introduced. Electric trains started to replace steam, and more electric trams were used. Factories used electricity to work machines and electrical goods like vacuum cleaners and washing machines became available to some people.

An advert for some of the earliest electric applicances.

Joyce

As well as gardening tools and other household items, my dad's shop also made and sold the new, electric 'wireless set'. During the school holidays my brother and I helped in the shop. We were allowed to sell firewood and batteries, and weigh out nails and screws. Here is a picture of the shop with the tricycle that was used for deliveries. This shop eventually had to be knocked down for the building of the M4 motorway.

HOME LIFE

HOUSEWORK

Most women did not work once they were married. They stayed at home and looked after their homes and families. Few households had electric machines in the thirties, so keeping the house clean took much longer than today and women often did housework all day.

Washing machines were rare and so clothes and sheets were washed by hand. They would then be put through a mangle to squeeze out the water. There were no tumble dryers so all laundry was hung outside to dry, or, if it was raining, around the stove.

Bob

My mum did not go out to work, but I remember she was always busy. On Mondays she did the washing in a large copper in the corner of the kitchen. Ironing was done with two steel irons that were heated up on the gas ring. Mum was always cooking - making jams or bottling fruit. She also made delicious bread, cakes and pies - her apple and blackberry tart was my favourite.

DOMESTIC STAFF

In the 1930s many people were employed as domestic staff in town houses. People in domestic service were often quite well looked after but had to work very hard. They usually had one half day off a week, and perhaps a weekend once a month.

Arthur

My family had three members of staff: a cook, a maid and a nanny. Cook was Irish, fat and very jolly. I never saw Cook use a recipe book, she just seemed to produce delicious meals out of her head. My brother and sisters and I used to sneak into the kitchen to see what she was baking. We were often chased out with a broom!

THEN & NOW

• In the thirties it would have taken a housewife most of the day to do the washing. Now it takes only a few minutes to fill and empty the machine.

SHOPPING

In the early 1930s few people had refrigerators so they had to shop every day. There were no supermarkets and most shopping was done at small local shops or at the market. Food was bought fresh or in cans or jars. There was no frozen food. Perishable goods such as milk, butter and meat had to be kept in ice bought from the fishmonger, or stored in a cool larder. Dried goods like flour, rice and biscuits did not come in packets, but were weighed out and wrapped in paper.

Fruit and vegetables were always bought fresh, often from a market stall.

Old Money

Before decimalization, British currency was made up of pounds, shillings and pence. There were twelve pence (12d) in a shilling (5p today), and twenty shillings (20/-) in a pound. There were many more types of coins and bank notes. There was a one pound note and a ten shilling (50p) note.

Many shops delivered to the door.

Joyce

*We lived **20** minutes away from the shops. Luckily the tradesmen called at home often. The baker came daily, the milkman several times a day and the greengrocer twice a week. Most produce was only available during the relevant season: fresh vegetables in the summer and fruits in the autumn. At other times of the year fruit and vegetables were bottled, dried or salted. In summer we waited for the ice cream tricycle to come by. The salesman rang a bell and called out 'Stop me and buy one.' My favourite ice cream was an orange snofrute. It cost one penny (less than ¹/2p) and came in a waxed cardboard wrapper.*

THEN & NOW

• In the 1930s a loaf of bread cost about 4d (less than 2p). Today a loaf costs between 40p and 80p.

• In 1931 a typical housewife spent £2 12s 6d (£2.63) a week, on housekeeping. Now it would cost her over £100.

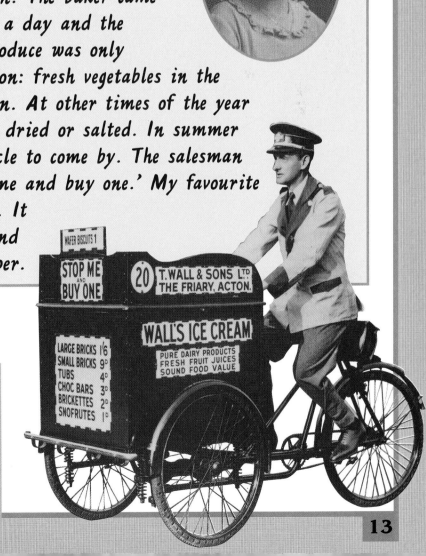

WAFER BISCUITS 1

STOP ME AND BUY ONE

20 T. WALL & SONS LTD
THE FRIARY, ACTON.

WALL'S ICE CREAM
PURE DAIRY PRODUCTS
FRESH FRUIT JUICES
SOUND FOOD VALUE

LARGE BRICKS 1'6
SMALL BRICKS 9ᴰ
TUBS 4ᴰ
CHOC BARS 3ᴰ
BRICKETTES 2ᴰ
SNOFRUTES 1ᴰ

SCHOOL

In the 1930s, children had to go to school from age 5 to 14. Most children went to mixed council schools, which had 3 classes: infants, juniors and seniors.

Bob

The teachers at my school were very strict. If you made a mistake in spelling or English, you had to write 100 lines of the thing you got wrong. Sometimes we were smacked on the head or whacked with a ruler across the hand. If you were really naughty, you were sent to the head master to be caned.

Classrooms were often dull. There were few bright posters on the walls, and the furniture was wooden or metal and very practical. Each child had his or her own desk facing the front of the class, and nobody was allowed to talk during lessons. Most time was spent on reading, writing and arithmetic.

This picture shows some of the boys from Bob's class in the playground. The girls played in a different playground!

EXERCISE

Schools did not have the playing fields or gyms that they do today. Games such as football would be played in the playground or at the local recreation ground.

Sheila

Saint David is the patron saint of Wales, and every year on 1 March, our school celebrated Saint David's Day by putting on a performance. Each class had to perform a concert piece. Here is my class' group photo. I am sitting in the centre.

LEAVING SCHOOL

Some children went on to grammar schools or the high school but most had to leave school at 14 to find work.

HEALTH

Healthcare in the thirties was not as good as it is today. There was no National Health Service and most visits to the doctor cost money, so poor people rarely saw a doctor.

Arthur

My mother insisted that fresh air was good for you. My brother and sister and I were dressed up and taken for a walk every day - whatever the weather!

Children did not have injections to protect them against childhood diseases and often got ill. When one child in a school class came down with an illness, the other children had to be put in 'quarantine' and were sent home for two weeks.

A nurse comforts a child in hospital.

TUBERCULOSIS

One very serious disease was tuberculosis or TB. This was very infectious and children who had it had to be kept apart from the other children.

Pasteurized milk was introduced which was supposed to prevent the spread of TB.

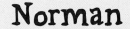

Norman

There was one classroom at our school with open sides and canvas screens where the tuberculosis children were taught. We never got to know them as they never mixed with the rest of the school.

This picture, showing Norman's sister, was a winning entry in a competition run by the dairy industry. They wanted to promote how healthy pasteurized milk was, and sponsored many 'Bonny Baby' competitions.

THEN & NOW

• In the 30s, the number of cases of measles reported was over 400,000 a year. Now there are less than 7,500 a year.

HAVING FUN

TOYS AND GAMES

Although children had far fewer toys in the 1930s they had fun making up their own games. Because there was so little traffic it was safe for children to play in the streets. Hopscotch squares were chalked onto the paving stones using different coloured chalks. Running with a hoop and stick was also a popular game. You had to see how long you could keep your hoop moving.

Joyce

My brother Dennis and I did not have many toys, so those we had were carefully treasured. These pictures show my dolls' house and my brother's clockwork tin-plate train set.

Norman

My sister and I enjoyed blowing bubbles. We dipped our bubble pipes into a tin of soapy water.

POCKET MONEY

Children spent their pocket money at the local corner shop. Sweets such as jelly babies, aniseed balls or dolly mixtures were sold from big glass jars. They were weighed out into 2oz, 4oz and 8oz (50g, 110g and 225g) measures. Other sweets like gob stoppers or sherbet dabs were sold from a penny tray or a half-penny tray.

COMICS

Comics such as the *Dandy* or the *Eagle* cost one penny. Children would often try and read a whole comic in the shop while the shopkeeper was busy with other customers, and then buy another one to take home!

The wireless

In 1936 the BBC started the first British television service, but since very few people had a television, not many were able to watch it. People got their entertainment by listening to the wireless. Wireless sets were quite expensive, costing about £20, but most homes had one.

Bob

We had a dome-shaped wireless made of Bakelite, an early sort of plastic. It had two batteries, one was a dry battery and the other was an accumulator wet battery that needed recharging. It was my job to take the accumulator to a wireless shop for charging.

▶ Gracie Fields was a very well known singer in the 1930s.

CINEMA

The cinema was a popular form of entertainment in the thirties. On Saturday mornings the cinemas opened for children only. Children called this 'Saturday morning pictures'. The programmes only cost one penny (less than $^1/_2$p) and children queued to watch films like *Tarzan* or a weekly serial such as *Flash Gordon*.

THEN & NOW

- A cinema show in the thirties consisted of two movies and a newsreel. Now they usually show just one film.

- Cinemas then had only one screen, there were no multiplexes.

The first full length Disney film to be made was *Snow White and the Seven Dwarfs*.

In 1938 Walt Disney started making colour cartoons. Mickey Mouse was the star of the first cartoon to have words and music and has been a children's favourite ever since.

HOLIDAYS

Holidays were rare for most people in the thirties. People couldn't afford them, transport was difficult and nobody had paid leave from work until 1938.

Norman

In 1935, 'school journeys' were introduced by the government. They were holiday breaks for children who would not otherwise ever have a holiday. Often children would be sent to stay on a farm in the country.

Our school went on one such holiday in 1937. We went to East Sussex. These pictures show us visiting Bodiam Castle and having fun at the Hastings swimming baths.

The Beach

People who could take holidays or day trips usually went to the beach. Brighton, Blackpool, Southend and Skegness were popular resorts.

Joyce

*Our luggage was always sent on in advance for our holidays. The trunks would be marked with a large label saying **PLA** which stood for Passenger Luggage in Advance. They were collected by the horse-drawn van of the Southern Railway Company and taken to the station to be put on a train to Dorset where we spent our holidays.*

People dressed very formally on the beach. Unless they were swimming, men kept their suits and caps on! Most people just paddled - not many had ever learned to swim. Children enjoyed their days on the beach playing cricket, making sand castles and watching Punch and Judy shows.

Sheila

We had relatives who lived in a pretty seaside village in Pembrokeshire. We sometimes took short holidays there. This picture shows me and my family on the beach.

Norman

The first holiday I went on was to the Isle of Wight. We travelled there by train. When we got to the

island, we stayed in a boarding house. This picture shows my family, plus a few other holiday makers in an open-topped coach known as a 'charabanc'. Every day the charabanc would take people off on day trips around the island.

BUTLIN'S HOLIDAY CAMPS

In 1936 Billy Butlin opened the first Butlin's holiday camp in Skegness. It was a totally new way to have a holiday. You paid a single price which covered food, accommodation and entertainment.

The Holiday You'll Never Forget!

BUTLINS SKEGNESS HOLIDAY CAMP

THEN & NOW

- When Billy Butlin's first holiday camp opened, a week there cost £2. Today it would cost between £50 and £100.

24

Arthur

My family had a boat which we kept on the west coast of Scotland. She was **60** feet (**20m**) long, but was by no means the largest on the Clyde in those days. We had many happy holidays sailing amongst the islands. Two fishermen acted as crew and my brother and sisters and I enjoyed helping them. Great care had to be taken with the huge sails to prevent them getting mildew. The boat was very well cared for with well-scrubbed decks and shiny polished brassware.

Arthur's early love of sailing led to him joining the Royal Navy when he left school.

TRANSPORT

HORSE-DRAWN VEHICLES

The 1930s was probably the last decade when horse-drawn traffic was still a common sight to see. Small companies often used horse-drawn vehicles to deliver goods locally.

Bob

This picture shows the horse and wagon that my dad used to deliver goods from my grandfather's hardware shop. The horse was used until the early thirties when it was replaced with a van.

Towards the end of the thirties, vans started to take the place of horse-drawn transport.

A Leicester milk van in 1938.

TRAMS

Few people had cars at the beginning of the 1930s. Short journeys like shopping or going to school were made on foot or by bicycle. Longer journeys were made by bus, tram or train.

Every big town had a tram service. Trams were a curious mixture of both trains and buses. They ran on metal rails laid down the middle of most streets, but were directed by policemen, like buses and other traffic.

Arthur

Glasgow was famous for its tram system. The trams got their power from electric wires overhead. When the tram reached its destination, it did not turn around. The driver walked from the front to the back carrying his throttle and brake handles, and the back end now became the front. I travelled to school by tram - the fare was one penny. Children often jumped on and off trams while they were moving. The conductor did not seem to mind, and often helped haul you on board.

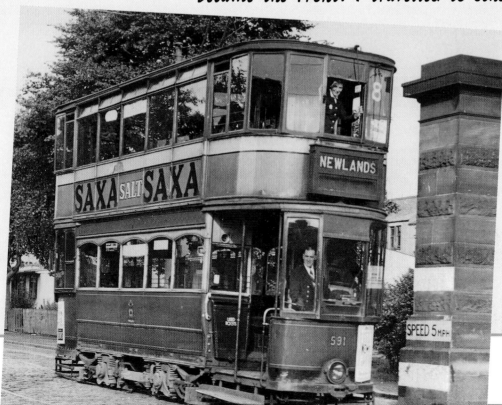

BIKES

For many people in the thirties, the bicycle was the only form of transport. Children cycled to school and many people cycled to work. Most postmen and policemen did their jobs by bike.

Joyce

My family did not have a car of their own but my grandparents had a beautiful car. It was an Armstrong Siddeley and it was a great treat to go for a ride in it.

CARS

By the end of the decade, cars were being mass-produced in Britain. Austin, Morris, Triumph and Rover were some of the early makes. Although cars were fairly cheap, a new car was still too expensive for most families.

THEN & NOW

- A new family car cost between £100 and £200 in the thirties. Now a similar sized car would cost over £10,000.

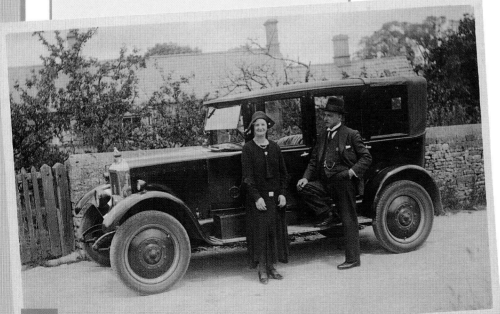

BOATS

Passenger boats were often powered by steam. A steamship was a huge liner that could carry over a thousand people. A trip to America took at least four days.

Arthur

When we went on holiday we went by paddle steamer. The steamer was powered by steam from coal-fired boilers. The engine room was full of a wonderful array of shiny copper pipes, pumps and pistons. It was fun to watch when the steamer was arriving or leaving a pier, because the engineers had to reverse the huge pistons. At this time you could see inside the paddle boxes and it was like looking into a huge washing machine.

THE SECOND WORLD WAR

On Sunday 3 September 1939, people crowded around their wireless sets to hear Prime Minister Neville Chamberlain speak to the country. He said, 'I have to tell you that this country is now at war with Germany.' People had been expecting a war for more than a year and many thought air raids and gas attacks would begin straight away.

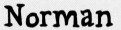

Norman

On the 4 September 1939, the day after war was declared, my mother and sister and I left London to stay with my aunt Pauline in Bournemouth. Everyone was very worried that London would be bombed. In fact nothing happened until the next year and so we all returned home after a few weeks. People came to call this the 'phoney war'. This picture shows us walking along the front in Bournemouth.

After the initial worry and panic, the war actually started very quietly and there was no fighting until the summer of 1940. However, the decade came to an uneasy end with many young men leaving home to fight in the Second World War, and with their families not knowing when or if they would return.

FURTHER READING

History From Objects - *At School, In the Street, Keeping Clean* and *Toys*, Hodder Wayland

History From Photographs - *Clothes and Uniforms, Houses and Homes, Journeys, People Who Help Us, School, In the Home* and *In the Street*, Hodder Wayland

Take Ten Years - *1930s*, Evans Brothers 1991

20th Century Fashion -*20s and 30s, Flappers and Vamps*; Cally Blackman, Heinemann, 1999

Travelling in Grandma's Day, Faye Gardner, Evans Brothers 1997

Fiction:
The Family from One End Street, Eve Garnett, Puffin

GLOSSARY

accumulator: A type of rechargeable battery used in early wirelesses.

boarding house: An inexpensive hotel, usually at the seaside.

copper: A large bowl, originally made of copper, with a fire underneath, that was used for doing the laundry.

council: A local governing organization.

decimalization: The introduction of a new system of money in 1971.

ironmonger: A shop selling tools, building materials and household implements.

mangle: A machine with rollers for squeezing water out of wet laundry.

National Health Service: A service set up in 1948 which aimed to give free health care to everybody.

pasteurization: The sterilization of milk by heat.

perishable goods: Foods that are likely to decay quickly.

power station: A place that generates electricity, often from burning coal.

quarantine: A period of isolation to prevent the spread of illness.

shilling: An amount of money worth 12 old pence (5p).

slum housing: Very poor or run-down housing.

suburbs: The area of housing outside a city centre.

tuberculosis: A dangerous and infectious disease.

unemployed: Without a job.

wireless: A radio set.

INDEX